The Traffic
of the
Heart

Poems by
Miranda Panaretou-Cambanis

Carolina Wren Press

© Copyright, 1986, Carolina Wren Press
Cambanis, Miranda Panaretou, 1944–
  I. Title.
PS3553.A428T73   1986   811'.54   85-26594
ISBN 0-932112-22-6 (pbk.)

Some of these poems first appeared in the following publications: *Hyperion Poetry Journal, St. Andrews Review,* and *The Archive.*

By the same author: *The Execution* (a play)
Thorp Springs Press, 1975.

Cover Photo "Rock Formations" by Alexis Cambanis

Publication of this book is made possible in part by a grant from the North Carolina Arts Council.

I want to thank everybody who made this book possible and especially the following people:

My son, Alexis Cambanis, who took both pictures that appear in the book, and my son, Thanassis Cambanis, whose sense of the ridiculous never failed to amuse and help me.

My friends: Judy Hogan, who never gave up hope about getting a complete manuscript from me;

Daphne Athas, who always encouraged and supported my writing;

Gucki Obler, who did all the typing, often, in the middle of the night, without complaining;

Martha Arnold, who worked hard to convince me that English *is* indeed different from Greek and I should try to keep it separate; and

Stamatis Cambanis, who made it possible for me to have the time to write and finish this book.

My gratitude goes to all of you.

Dedicated to the memory of my father,
Athanassios Panaretos,
who chose to be good,
not happy.

Contents

Preface

Miranda Cambanis came to the United States in 1967 and has lived here since then, going back and forth between Chapel Hill, Athens, and Paros. One of the generation of university students who spearheaded the resistance against the dictatorship of 1967–74, she has published plays and poems about the experience of living in the two mutually exclusive worlds of Greece and the United States.

The poems in this collection speak to us from the place where a man may go who, as Elytis says, is nothing else but a man. They are poems about family: father, mother, getting married, childbirth, old age; about Greece and America; about women; and about the emotions of condemnation, grief, estrangement, anger, pride and hope. Conceived and written in English, their tradition is the 20th century Greek poetic one, which has flourished for two decades although it has only begun to be recognized in Europe and America since the translations of Cavafy, Solomos and Palamas and the Nobel prizes awarded to Seferis and Elytis. But Cambanis' point of departure is the exile in America. There is no category for a Greek experience of America covering the protest of the Sixties through the upgraded philistinism of the Eighties, and no reliable sounding board in the pop-Zorba, Americanized Greece. These are poems of exile.

In the United States we have as many realities as there are aliens, and while we pay lip-service, we all too often believe the frontiers of the psyche to lie in outerspace. This is a mechanical vision. We are unconscious of the messages inside our borders. Our immigrants have long since sloughed off their true knowledge and grabbed onto identification with the America of the tight backbone, closed mouth, private grief and understated anger, where even a joke must be told with a straight face. Our penchant for large and public systems has led straight to personal uncertainty.

It is into this abyss that these poems rush. They must be cherished for the fearlessness with which they express the honor of the naked heart. Lowered expectations bring no sense of defeat. Although much is shown as ignoble, nothing is small. Love is blood. Cambanis talks out of what she calls the 'loser's skin,' feeling everything, knowing nothing, and recognizing the 'undefinable more of the gods.' As an exile she takes advantage of 'being a target in the eye of the wind.' As a 'ridiculer of the good fairies' she contemplates the ideas of feelings and destiny, and of permanence and hope. 'Events leave us behind, youth is turned to rust and the security of childhood has long anchored itself in memory.'

Her deepening vision ranges from curdling contempt, those conversations between the Parthenon and the Statue of Liberty—"Your illness is very peculiar, Madame, you must undoubtedly be a foreigner"—to passionate declaration: "I don't want to live like this. . . This is where I begin to fight without predictions."

Passion is liberation. The territory is partly political, always personal. Some lines disconcert and may be an invasion. But their style is legato and such a paradox compels. It is rare in a world which deems emotion irrelevant and sensation, information and idea to be the reliable coin, to fall under this spell. In this book, emotion is honor. The corollary is that the human state is beyond hope or despair. For us who have made a country where computers use the shorthand once reserved for God and where our destruction is droned into intercoms, such passion is so wondrous, we can hardly believe it, and if we do, we who so long for it, it renders us helpless.

To make the gesture of 'No' in Greece a person doesn't shake the head from left to right, but lifts the face toward the sky and rolls the eyes up into the head till the pupils disappear and only the whites are left. The most famous 'No' in modern times was this gesture engraved as the word 'Ochi' upon a mountain which the Italians faced on their march into Greece from Albania in 1940. It signalled their defeat. In a similar way these poems arrest us and we are suddenly contemplating hope as "the last moment" and going with it. Miranda Cambanis has made a lifetide which strips and, in the stripping, gives forth life.

Daphne Athas
Chapel Hill, NC
1985

Poetry

Poetry lives in perpetual insomnia
and not in damp houses with leaking roofs and hungry children
as has often been said between well paid intellectuals at cocktail parties,
wishing, in their drunkenness, to be poets with any other voice
except their own.
In these times of distress and improvisation,
when some are killed for only one night and others for an eternity
they don't even want to know,
poetry lives in perpetual insomnia and stays away from sleeping pills
or promises of eternity or poems about herself.
Poetry is thin, with dark eyes and a hollow face that echoes all
the time without distinction. The distinction lies in her breasts that
are full of beat under her vague dress that changes colors according to the
        statements.
She never fails, grows old or dies but simply moves to the next place
when it is time to move, to slap, to love, to incorporate the unspoken
before it fades away unrecognized.
When poetry sleeps, she is fatally wounded. Her breasts lie still under
her red dress and her voice surrenders to inarticulate shrieks that freeze
the tears and put a gun on the temple of those who reject their own
heartbeat and believe they can cross reality when they can only lift it.
Poetry comes quickly to us, all of us, as a sin and as ecstasy
without preparation or purpose or continuity, like a stray bullet from
the guts of a rock that managed to speak after centuries of silence.
Poetry does not protect herself but moves in and out of pain like a warrior
and like a woman who lost all of her sons in violence and is still
going through the shadows erect, strong and justified, without hope and without
        death.
Poetry is the voice of those who refuse to forget their isolation,
and so she lives in perpetual insomnia, like a captive snake before it
surrenders.

Life, Half-Mast

We never raised our voice much
or our hand
or our flag so that it could be seen by everybody.
We simply lowered our expectations.

Letters from My Father

Freedom starts when guilt is over

Prologue

That night,
June 21, 1967,
my father waited for me at the door
without his jacket,
the sleeves of his white shirt rolled up.
I had never seen him like that before.
His face was red and hot;
yet, he was shivering
and his feverish eyes,
almost unfamiliar,
were holding something that
was either fear or triumph—
I couldn't tell.
He motioned me to his study
and, as he sat in his favorite chair
—the one with the straight back—
he asked me for a cigarette.
(My father had not smoked for thirty-five years.)
I stood in front of him with screaming blood, waiting
for what seemed twenty-four years
(my whole life until then),
before he spoke.

"I am losing my mind,"
he said quietly.
"I couldn't find my way home
this afternoon.
I had to ask somebody for directions.
Mine will be a slow death
and I want to apologize now
while I know who you are
and who I am."

And without giving me any chance for words,
he was gone
leaving his half smoked cigarette behind:
his entire loneliness.

Letters from My Father

I

My daughter,
I hope America will be good to you
because I know you won't be good to her.
It takes you so long to forgive indirectness
and you always hated limp, inhibited handshakes.
To be good doesn't mean to be happy.
I know that well
and what's worse, you know it, too,
even though I tried so hard
to stress the virtues of both,
only to be left with the disguise
of being happy.
But you saw too clearly, too much, too often.
"Happiness is one defense that always sinks,"
you wrote in your journal—
that I read secretly one night—
when I thought you were asleep.
You were out, being happy—not good—
and it took you two whole days to sink.

Nothing is the same since you left.
A strange fog is slowly permeating my brain.
It doesn't hurt,
but it's confusing when I think of all the years
that are stored up there
waiting to amount to something
bigger than my will
or my capacity for remembrance.

The corner café has closed down.
What's the use of sadness, hate
(or lack of it),
the collections of unused silver, dusty antiques, still butterflies,
the gold teeth in the twisted mouth,
the candleholders on each side of my silence,
the aspirins and their temporary relief?

My daughter,
freedom starts when guilt is over.

Don't send any more postcards.
Just bring back what you took with you:
The permanence of an understanding.

II

I know it will make you sad to hear that
we had to move:
Your childhood is turning into
impersonal apartment buildings
with big cement mouths
that eat up memories indiscriminately.
The fog in my head
moved with me.
I don't mind it.
It doesn't hurt.
It makes me forget
even you, sometimes.
There is not enough light
in the rooms of this new house
but your mother says it's because
I keep turning it off.
Maybe I always wanted to be in the dark
because I saw so much
against my will,
that the will broke
into thousands of splinters
and nobody, except me, sees that as a relief.

I can't remember if I was ever young,
but your mother says I was born old
because, those days, there was no
advantage in being young.
I don't know.
It's too quiet here with just the two
of us trying to guess all that remains unspoken.
I never feel like talking any more
except to myself,
in front of the mirror,
so I won't forget how.
I whistle sometimes.
I count the cars that go by.
I constantly try to remember something:
perhaps the password to what's left of my life.

The ocean between us
has stopped roaring.

III

I have moved on as long as I possibly could.
I am getting tired
and the nights become longer and longer
in this sleepless vacuum
that used to be a human being,
your father,
me.
It's neither fair nor dignified
to evoke only pity and resentment
instead of love.
It erases your whole life
and turns it into a bitter territory
where hope has no place, or reason.
I will no longer be dependent
on anybody's grace.
I will not be thirsty, hungry, or afraid.
My daughters are gone.
I want to rest.
There are a few threads left:
weave them into Mercy.

Don't cry:
I know you'll get here in time.

Conversations between the Parthenon and the Statue of Liberty

Sleeplessness

I shouldn't cry any more now that I'm left with this red shawl in my hands to rest
    my cheeks on.

At 4 o'clock in the morning all the way from Greece,
your voice splits the night in half
with screams and curses for the madness of distance
and with words of love that are always urgent.
At 4 o'clock in the morning I'm still going
as if I have just begun or just ended–nothing in between.
The difference lies in the color of the heartbeat.
I shall no longer run the dusty streets with a child swelling in my veins.
I can't give up my memories, yet they cut so vertically through me
that I am always half.
I lie down to sleep and have no sleep.
I see it: nobody can enter my body now.
The friends and the lovers are all pushed aside
as if scorched and rusted by their own lies.
Used to the light, my eyes starve for the darkness of the unexplored space
between two sheets still warm by a vague presence.
My body has the weight of fear;
weight controlled by whispers.

The Doctor

Your illness is very peculiar,
    Madame.
You must undoubtedly be a foreigner . . .
In *this* country, the symptoms
are like an open book
deciphered,
        simple, and
            not quite as crooked.
I can deal with sex,
        insanity,
            or weight,
but for your case, it's kind of late.
Our education is not particularly concerned
    with soul, I'm afraid,
and I honestly, Madame, hate to see myself
    paid
but it's an affluent society
and although we can cure all diseases with
    pills of morality,
we cannot prescribe salvation freely
    because of the taxes
that limit our humanitarian process
    like iron axes.
Doctors suffer a lot
    in *this* country, Madame. . . .
Oh, incidentally, did you say you
    believe you suffer from
        l-o-n-e-l-i-n-e-s-s?
Here is your bill—what a confusing illness!
You must undoubtedly be a foreigner.
    How do you spell it, Madame?

At the A & P

Impersonal, pale, middle class women
who breathe through the rollers of their hair—choking,
and believe in what should have been
without fighting what is,
who occasionally buy little pieces of their heart
at the cheapest cost
often with little square coupons carefully cut out of the local paper that they read
      religiously (in case they see a name they know),
comparing prices, children, boredom, psychiatrists, recipes,
the inadequacy of Friday night sex,
perceiving the world through the rolled-up windows
of their air-conditioned station wagon
(the ultimate in practicality and transportation of the family depression)
a baby in the back and the dog in the front
to protect the nonexistent virginity of their narrow horizon
that's never shattered by lightning,
because lightning is not easy and burns the body at its center completely,
with no discounts or trade ins,
or acts of good will that lead to more and more nowheres
more empty nights
more suicides
more agony
less and less love.

                                          Airport Road A & P, Chapel Hill

Studies for Self-Improvement

So, you, too, exiled yourself
for studies and a brighter future.
I remember you
(before your voluntary burial)
as I remember my mother's tears for mine.
You didn't have a mother
but you loved some pale, skinny theologist
"with virtues"
who expected to see white doves of purity
fly through your hands
that he never held between his
limp, sweaty fingers,
busy, as they were, leafing the gospel
like we leaf a daisy:
no, God didn't love him
and eventually, neither did you.

So, here you are, alone,
for studies and a brighter future
in this country of opportunity
with Columbus' example
to motivate your every struggle.

Well, good luck, as they say here
and a happy return to the homeland,
which will undoubtedly disappoint you
after so many golden years of
sporty stimulation and learning.
Your English is excellent.
If only you had something to say
with it!

Good Friday

Austere Good Friday, the linen shroud of the old
spread over the lilac blossoms
like determined mist
eating through the chanted paganism
of the Holy Week
and through the spine of my heart.

It rained hard all morning
straight drops
like calculated lines with no destiny
that cut across the stone with the steady pace of sorrow.
My mood changed from Bach to gray to flute to black
where it stayed
accompanied by the silent bells of mourning.

Second-Hand Shop

How this time has passed, my love,
How my life has passed . . .

Long days, far away, bent,
surrendered to red darkness
extinguished lights, closed eyes,
memory open to temporary games,
uneven, lost,

dirty pages of a meaningless book
stripped of words or photographs,
small book, infected,
exposed in the window
of this foreign second-hand shop
that sells without buying
the pride of my sadness . . .

Statement, Apology, Self-Deposition or, Simply, a Farewell

And I am still the same where it matters
where it hurts
where my resistance bent but didn't surrender
where stalactites replaced tears
and transparent patches of memory mended the cracks
and restored their wholeness in bronze.

I am still the same, like before,
tracing your eyes from wave to leaf
from womb to heart
with the same frenzy, the same curiosity
tracing your hair, so demanding and mythical
like roots leading to the body of my body
and your hands resting with tenderness
on my tormented face that insisted on recapturing
the twisted mouth of the woman who cried,
"We are being orphaned in our own soul for nothing,"
that Sunday afternoon in Constitution Square
crowded with bored tourists who glanced at the spectacle annoyed
and filled more colored postcards
with ethereal descriptions about the Attic sky
that was dripping blood . . . .

I am still the same where it matters
where it hurts most
where it all remains undefined, yet known
with you and you and you chained
and the echo of my voice saying,
what life is this
what life
scattered between yield and stop signs
what life, where, abandoned in separations that
do not defy distance
do not stretch love beyond its surface
what life is this
slowly moving in spaces without contents
without doors, timeless
without history other than that of the stale intellect
continuously trying to avoid construction,
this whole country in the mercy of shiny, automatic bulldozers

with one lane always closed to crossing
and the multiple direction streets
leading to more and more credit centers,
what life, how, how much more oxygen
can our lungs produce before our choices are choked to death
what life, what death
we all live on borrowed premises.

I am more mellow now, without limits,
with a grey that finally revealed the sea
the sea that kept me in her thighs burning but not consuming
and engraved my identity in the ribs of the cypress
with a brine that is no longer bitter.

I am more mellow now, more concrete
measuring distances with anger for distorting
priorities and pride
measuring love with gigantic leaps
through airports and letters written on lined paper
to avoid confusion
establishing solitude as the one language
that will never be foreign . . . .

I am still the same then,
All of my alien documents hold me intact:
black and white photograph, austere,
place of birth, color of eyes, date of birth
number of exits, number of entries,
number of hopes.
My eyes are still blue but sleepless.
My face recognizes yours
and states the unspoken
that holds me erect and wounded.

I can contain you now,
all of you
I can touch you without regrets, compromise or fear,
I know my hands, I trust them:
the aging pain of their fingers
define my continuity.

I am still the same where it hurts
at my center that defeated death

still the same
knowing and wanting to know to want.
Beyond their redness
my eyes are still blue
beyond the understanding of the cause
my senses are turned like antennas of silk
towards the Greek pelago
that never talks, only listens. . . .

I am still the same.
My nakedness is unassuming
The black veil of mourning, removed.
Miles past the silence of the Statue of Liberty
I can feel the softness of the marble
penetrating my body.
My sons beside me
restlessly anticipate the explosion of the red geraniums
and accept my agony as an answer.
I am all nerves but stronger: more mellow in my darkness

And I am coming home.

Jogging

Where are they all going
when they pass you by,
sweating and panting
with alarming blankness in their eyes?
They jog their life away
and even *that* lacks intensity.
They jog with systematic,
unemotional steps,
same way they have to have three meals a day
and always supper at 6:00
(otherwise, they might have to improvise
something different to fill the time at home).
Before they even get the chance to think
of what they ate
or of the person who bothered to fix it,
the dishes get put away quickly
because the news is starting
and mother has weight watchers meeting
to make sure she lost her half pound
of self-indulgent fat.
Light reading follows:
the paper, some gardening or anti-smoking
literature, perhaps,
(the tobacco merchants are finally getting
what they deserve and we can take clear lungs
to the grave).

This sudden preoccupation
with healthier bodies and longer lives
is as ludicrous as their priorities
which always start in the house
they'll be paying off till they die in it
or be put in a rest home to die remembering it.
They always had these bodies
but didn't know what to do with them.
They produced children – lots of them
since God said so and they spend
so many Sundays socializing in His
suburban house.
After that, the bodies became limp
sitting through long hours of violent

or non-sensical television shows,
executive and academic meetings,
unanimated discussions with whomever`
they felt they should have them.
The men read the sports section:
they worry when the piano starts
in the next room:
"Do you think our son is effeminate, dear?
He is not into sports at all and he hates basketball.
I read an article in *Playboy* about it.
I must ask my psychiatrist next time,
don't you think?"

Meanwhile, the jogging continues
through traffic, parks, squares, bedroom floors;
self-righteous health institutions pop up
in every block
with a permanent smell of broccoli
and unwashed repression
(vegetables never thought of themselves
as reformers until now).
The President advises
better eating for longer living (not better)
because they all have a lot to do:
they have to mow the lawn regularly
or else the symmetry will be broken;
keep all the "different" people out of their
neighborhoods so the prices can stay healthy, too,
and the children can keep on living in
their all-white fantasy world until
they are eighteen
when they, too, can start
jogging their disillusionment away
while they pursue useful studies
so they won't have to become like uncle Eddy
who ended up selling furniture
(even though he prospered more than any
of them and he is happy—
unlike them.)

The old do not jog
because they are neatly put out of sight
in wheelchairs that move as slowly as their

remaining years.
They have nothing to run away from
except, perhaps, from those who put them there,
their own children,
who find their unseen longevity "fantastic"
and think of Alzheimer's as a German chain store
that has finally come to this country
to help their parents find their lost equilibrium
so they can finally take that trip to Europe
they've been wanting to take since college
without having to worry about the weekly
Sunday visits.

Where are they all going
when they pass you by,
sweating and panting
with alarming blankness in their eyes?
What images, what sequences, what justifications
will ever fill these long lives till death?

Blue Guide—An Extra Page

You can't see Greece at $5.00 a day any more.
Greeks have picked up the worst from the
multitudes of tourists
instructed to drool over the Parthenon marble,
corroding it
in self-righteous admiration
that is never expressed in Greek
(they all had it in college, of course, but
their own language is so much easier!).
Now, you get charged for a glimpse of the sky
that's no longer blue,
or the sea that has turned grey, black,
misty, hostile
protesting the invasions of the fleets,
the yachts, the submarines,
NATO, Enterprise with its crude, offensive contents,
Metro Goldwyn Mayer, the endless cruising. . . .

deprived of your ancient marble talismans
that fill the Museums of the world
time to demythologize Zorba the Greek in translation
and the cradle of democracy
—made of sturdy, American barbed wire—
that rocks anger and resentment
not romantic patriots;
time to revise the poetry of sunsets
on the Acropolis
half-eaten by pollution
(thank you, countries of the world, for offering
to rebuild the broken columns).
Sunsets that nobody has time for any more
since they coincide with Greek-speaking JR and
Kojak
on black and white televisions bought with
a month's wages.
Athens, fraudulent city,
shrouded in antennas of stupor
deprived of your ancient marble talismans
that fill the Museums of the world
but not your own.

The tourists keep coming.
They buy hundreds of post cards
and the myth of wine and dancing on the beach.
They try to assimilate Greece like ouzo
but don't know how to respond to either
the stripping of the soul
or the stripping of the body.

The effect is too sudden. The travel books didn't warn them.
They take endless close-ups of the landscape—
faces from a distance:
they are too emotional
too challenging
too dangerous
too unrefined and wrinkled
too clear in their hunger
too definite in their desire
too demanding in their sorrow.

They fill the beaches with their white, limp
bodies, chloroxed to death by their sanitary pools,
and look for Olympian gods
(mostly overweight these days)
who will trade dollars for love—of some kind.
Anything will do—let's not become too sentimental.
They are on vacation.
They have saved and earned their illusions.

Meanwhile,
the Greek nerves tick fiercely in the sun
that remains relentlessly loyal.
Their darkness overshadows the colors of
their cheap merchandise
spread out contemptuously
like a magnificently made-up whore
who understands everything but is no
longer willing.

Summer moves on
with its big, absolute nights
mixed with stars, sweaty skin, broken glasses,
wise lizards lying in front of new graves

and elderly snails on the park benches
leaving behind white lines of sperm and spit
like all the dead proclamations
of politicians and lovers.

The seasons have moved.
They have been pushed around by force.
Summer is sold out for another year.
The ships anchor.

The welcome signs are removed
The folding chairs are stacked away
tired, full of secrets and stains.

The tourists go home
with souvenirs, a few new words and a tan.

The Greeks return to their heart.

Return

We will all return one day
carefully selected among the
indifference of the four seasons.
We will get off the boat
in a straight line
hiding behind each other
(who will recognize us, any way?)
with memory as the only truth
that never betrayed us,
and knowing that nobody,
except the blind mathematician,
will be interested in our discovering
how to make the circles of pain square.
Our few belongings,
suitcases with letters,
black and white photographs of the past,
old loves,
will go through customs
unopened.

On the other side of the gate,
nobody will meet us.

Liquid Mirror

I can't speak with a mouth
full of acid,
neither can I balance myself
on slippery asphalt.

Eyes of the Water

I

And yes, I love you. I love you. I love. You.
As I felt you that glaring afternoon in May,
reaching down for the secrets of the water
that knew our reflections too well to speak.
I have loved before, seeking behind steel,
heavy doors,
people who took my hands for granted
and turned them against me, twisting my fate like demons.
I have loved in need,
been loved in guilt,
learning remorse's rage or the despair of colors
that turn dark
when you think them red and blooming and permanent.
"What is permanent is eaten up by itself,"
somebody said once,
getting up from the old, squeaky bed
with the indifference of the lover who
takes but doesn't know what or why:
the hunger of the overfed.

II

Tired of rented rooms, the heart wants to love for free
in houses with music and roots
because the heart lies beyond music and roots.
Now we are together. We have defeated the ocean
with the single, silver line of our bodies
that never rest, only love.

III

I said: "I will kill whoever touches you."
My passion always overwhelms you but we smile:
Your face opens like a sunflower to my eyes that you love
and I need your face for all these definitions
that insist on being vague through their incoherent balance.
"I come from different quarters," I whisper to your ear that
tastes softer than a leaf. "I am not from here, my blood runs
the streets of another land . . ."

Does it matter? Is it not the same heartbeat that knows no
boundaries? The same lightning in the embrace
that transforms us to crystal sails?
And the land an omen of the land?

Next to you, my fever reaches its source,
the same fever of the roots that cling to the ground of your womb
and tremble, and yield, and absorb the universe between us
reconfirming its center.

And yes, I love you. I love you. I love you.

Indigestion

Here we are
all three of us
you, he and I
talking, not talking
choking on gourmet bitterness
avoiding each other's eyes
excruciatingly comfortable in
this pink kitchen that makes me feel transient:
tension is sprouting snakes in my stomach
but I smile—
why do I feel like a part of the
furniture these days?

Afternoon in Slow Motion

This is a rusted spring
Angry
Quiet
Looking at me straight in the eyes
(that used to be soft)
without expectation
consequence
or reward.
The seasons hardly moved this year
they sat still, folded in their own shadow
blind, wingless, tired
without words of wisdom or enthusiasm.

And you, you, don't say, don't pronounce, don't . . . .
Leaving your house
in the crippled, unshaved afternoon,
I saw many dead
or maybe just reflections of a wish that constantly punishes me.
Nobody wants to die with a twisted smile on his face
but everybody wants a fair exchange with no deposit.
Bitter love, no love at all,
bitter mouth, no voice
sealed desires, put to sleep
fighting against the old statues
and the softness of that first spring.

From Body to Body

I said I would yield to a smile, to see where a mouth could lead me.
And from concession to concession
from smile to smile
from body to body
I have arrived here where death becomes one with my blood—
it takes my features
it wraps all around me
it breaks me in so many pieces that I can't recognize my own pulse
it makes me darker
it brings me to the final point
until neither silence can save me
nor honesty
nor you.

The Ballad of the Ashes

And so, you violated everything with the firmness of a dagger
straight to the heart, that regular, palpitating shape
we always choose to abuse out of habit or fear.
In front of a fire that moved slower than captivity,
you crossed out the heart completely
but crossed over to nothing
for there was nothing to cross
except for a decayed bridge of breathing bodies that resembled death
all so close to you, ready to suck you in their cold flames,
so close to you and yet, so distant from any actual measure of love
or visions we once thought we saw, way back, before the falling of the axe.
But most revelations evaporate, like quick storms that leave no traces anywhere,
unlike violations that somehow stay, mark, burn through surfaces, substance,
promises, harden the softness that struggles to exist in spite of itself,
abuse the tender spots and push the mouth way under water
with the cruelty of the executioner who wants to die for his sins but can't.
Without apparent recognition,
you chopped down time, space, making sacrilege legal,
a reason for destruction, a starting point perhaps
through channels full of monsters
dark and distorted, like faces in pain, printed with images of loss,
inside the alleys of their own blood that flew in and out of the night like
wounded sparrows looking for shelter in a hostile window.

We do spend our life behind windows, looking through the glass
before we open it, squinting our eyes and our souls,
choosing our path of sequence, our routine of death,
hiding behind our own reflection, using make-up as an excuse to look grotesque,
disguising our vulnerable weaknesses with barriers of glass,
forgetting how easily glass shutters once violated,
forgetting, always forgetting the horror of being forgotten,
separated from all the rest by a blackboard
we can't risk to erase and become unspoken of again,
a name written and forgotten, left in nothingness.
But I don't want to live like this. I don't want to accommodate my sadness.
I don't want to go hungry for all the things I believe I should have,
outside the reflection of solitude waiting for a knock on the door
or a glance from a stranger, any stranger to fill up the nights,
the empty spaces, the stretched out hands.
I don't want the purity that rises from the ashes, because ashes are ashes, burned
    continuity,

and only in poetry things come back to life whole after a sweeping fire.
And since we can't live with a future as unknown as all these flames that threaten
to leap at our dreams the minute we pronounce them,
and the past is lying somewhere between the ashes of a single night or maybe
    those of many nights,
we have to live with the present, its moment-to-moment step and its ashes,
proof of the world beyond the glass window, the world with its half-broken
mechanism that resists everything by declaring infinite despair.

But now I know where to begin. No more journeys. No plans. No more secret
    signs.
Violence, stronger than desire, tattoos my heart. No return.
This is where I begin to fight without predictions.

Your Name

Your name was the root that began at the
tenderness of my lips
with no fate other than that of being pronounced,
whispered and declared,
your name, that was meant to erase all the others
with a single breath, a single kiss.

Your name is the root that begins at the
tenderness of my lips
and returns to the loneliness of my lips, unspoken.

Last Attempt

I tell you, I have been through
The fire
  The ocean
    The bridges
Your eyes
  Your body
    Your fire
      Your ocean
        Your barriers – temporarily
Our pain – a state of siege
  Our fire
    Your distance
      Your resistance
        My persistence
Our dilemmas
  Their curiosity, indifference, coldness
My fire
  My tears
    My fears
      Our resentment
        Their jealousy
          My jealousy
My obsession, aggression, exasperation
  Your reluctance
    My adaptability to frightful nights
Your expulsion, expansion, levelling
  My oxidation, adoration, yearning
Our injuries, healing, immediacy
  My insatiability
  Their games
Your guilt, quick anger, affliction
  And again,
I have been through the poetry of your body
  the madness of your mouth
    the consumption of times that gave in
to nothing but purgatorial passion
suffering the continuous sunstroke of a dream
that came so close to the actual surface of love
so close to the dawn of things we once
raised above our limitations,
banners of light and water
undefined but living

a love that pulled its anchor high up
ignoring our urgency to go with it
leaving us with the strange reflection
of mist
and a wave of green blood
smooth but unfamiliar
   Illusive wound
surrounded by the darkness of our separate faces
ah love, fermented love of one single moment
that never accepted itself
   got attacked by hungry wolves

   and surrendered.

Liquid Mirror

I

Habit wore out the colorful wrapping of our love,
and inside, threatening, half-open
Pandora's box was waiting.
The mythical gifts, now squashed,
handed to us through catapultic letters
erased the light from the motion that was ours.
Expectations, strangled, filled the distance between us:
silence and absence. . . .
I can't speak with a mouth full of acid
neither can I balance myself on slippery asphalt
with thirty-seven years of omens on my back
and a line of sibyls to predict the end.

II

No more "Yes, we will."
No more.
Just that. No more. There is no door left to open lightly.
No more. "That's your word," you'd say, with sweat
still all over our bodies. But no more.
None of the promises sown in beds of bronze and blue
ever came of age.
We were always baptized in fear and rage
for everything we didn't dare,
passengers of a dream that capitulated.

III

Now, your absence certifies stillness,
our six years, two broken coffee cups
    faded from the rain.

Portraits of Women

*Her wounds had been pawned for nothing,
for a river that never overflowed,
a clumsy twist of the knife.*

Wedding

She got dressed quietly
wearing the new confusion
with the long, white, lace tear.

Night—so that the make-up would
cover the cracks perfectly.

Then, she disappeared
in the other side of herself

Alone. With the man
and with her memories.

Birth

The child was born at nine.
It was a very difficult birth.
The woman suffered violently, as usual.
The man got angry for having to wait so long.
The father-in-law cursed because it was not a boy.
The doctor presented the bill with polite boredom.
The nurses were giving information for the newborns.

The woman died quietly at ten, not as usual.
It was a very easy death.
The man got angry because she did not ask him.
The father-in-law cursed for the unexpected expenses.
The doctor signed the death certificate hurriedly.
The nurses looked at the child with pity.
And the child, that was not a boy,
    breathed regularly,
    without nightmares.

Child Prodigies

Well, it's true:
child prodigies
very rarely realize the predictions
of the proud parents and relatives
who live only for the future
ignoring the present of these living wonders
whose mental indigestion
starts too early to be treated.

From all those boys in the children's choir
we heard on the island
that phantasmagoric Christmas night, years ago,
(all very talented and beautiful)
none evolved as expected:
not one of them became a cherub
or even a second-rate angel.
I still remember their eyes
completely in love with the ethereal sky,
their pimples
and themselves.

As I heard, they all grew up, fat and wealthy,
they circumcised their dreams,
shrank up their halo in the dryer of routine
    (much easier than glory)
and slowly wore themselves out
in anonymity
among us
without one prodigious surprise
other than that of their death.

The first decade

When she hurts, he yawns.
Wherever she turns, he has already been.
When she insists, he withdraws.
When she cries, he is silent
and goes to sleep because she is so hysterical
that he can't cope.
She remembers how he never knew much
about first aid or second or third
in spite of all the books about emergencies
he read instead of talking to her.

When she stumbles, he tells her how she
ought to wear her glasses
and lectures her about perfect balance
that requires discipline
(God, those monotonous lectures that
are only voice, never heart).

When she moans, he turns up the music
(but when she is cheerful, he turns it down—
   what will the neighbors say?
   We didn't move to the suburbs to become
      gossip items!)
When sorrow overcomes her, he goes
to the movies, or the office, or
his lover:
when will she ever understand that he
has needs, too?

Contemporary Living

We disarmed ourselves
grew up
asked the palm readers for prophesies and answers
put our future inside parentheses
and our heart on ice
and decided that was progress.

However,
we still marry
sacrifice to traditional altars
seek our solutions in the innocence of children
paint our houses
with shiny but cheap plastic idealism
and continue to watch the six o'clock news
so we can have some topic of conversation
in case it's needed.

Silver Anniversary

It was the first time
in 25 years
they apologized to each other,
    sincerely, they thought.

However, that was all they had to say,
looking away from each other's eyes.

An Interesting Love Affair

He said:
>   We'll meet in New York.
>   It would be a mistake to die
>   without having seen what would undoubtedly be
>   considered as the Eighth Wonder
>   (if somebody had been sensible enough
>   to promote it to a wonder...).

She said:
>   But I love you.
>   I don't want to be loved in a noisy Mausoleum.

He said:
>   We'll make love in New York.
>   A red-lighted exit,
>   comfortable air-conditioning
>   and perfumed elevators
>   are part of everything there.
>   You'll be happy in New York.

She said:
>   I have gotten tired of exits
>   for they choke choice to death;
>   I prefer the human warmth to the
>   artificial,
>   and smelly staircases make the destination
>   more deserved.

He said:
>   I can only love you in New York
>   where seven million people
>   will fill the tank of my aloneness—
>   in case of accident, of course.

She said:
>   I could love you anywhere
>   but not enough
>   to try to cure the seven million aloneness
>   before my own.
>   You see, I have waited for the human touch too long
>   to be able to become a foreigner
>   in love. . . .

Post College

Early morning she drives to the office
punches the yellow card promptly
moves the rolling chair in front of the typewriter
adjusts her hair, her cheeks, her fingernails
blinks last night's big dreams
into the vacuum of the day
orders her mouth into smiling position
assumes a gracefully subservient posture
unbuttons the top button of her imitation silk, permanent press blouse
takes her vitamin tablets for the day
and, watching her slim reflection in the glass door,
wishes it were already 5:00 pm
next year, when a change might perhaps occur.

Parting

Listen:
I am going to leave you.
The green hope I had planted in your heart
turned yellow.

Unexpected autumn, that
of your closed face.
You keep smoking
and playing the same record:
"Even though I love you,
I can't have you."
The truth is, you can have me but you can't love me.

The music became louder,
the rain,
the desire
but the attempts of our fingers
to hold what was slipping away,
weakened with every kiss.

Outside the window,
we can see
castrated stars
faceless dreams
regrets.

Wedding Certificate

". . . All we need for the success
of our marriage," she wrote,
"is your signature.
Everything else will come with time."

Hundreds of signatures
under the kisses
and the squeezed desires
        – on paper –
marked her amputated world
of piled promises
for return
and "eternal" love.

Except for him,
everything else came with time. . .

Intercourse

This poem is for you, Maria,
the priest said
crossing himself with reverence
before leaving his semen
on her gold and silver chastity
warm, behind the crystal barrier
of the icon,
The Woman.

Guilt

I keep waiting for the day
you will stand before me,
your light blue uniform hanging on you
expressionless, bitter,
all of your edges eaten up by electricity
and needles that reduced you to negation
and you will ask without tenderness,
not like a child any more but like a woman
—what did you do with my blood
how could you forget me
how could you re-invest your soul
how could you let your ocean flow
inside some other shell
how dared you become somebody else's wound
and turn your face away,
how could you....

And I will say nothing
watching the rain fall on the marble shoulders
of the women in the square
who scream their pain at nights
through sealed, solitary lips.

Classical Study

I

She roamed the rooms in tactful resignation
looking for something she had missed before
a small something
smaller than instinct
a little more defined than happiness
a little less demanding than love
like a newspaper clipping
a receipt of stolen time
an old certificate of grandeur
something to make sense
to hang onto without guilt
something to justify the dignity of repression
the list of drastic changes that turned yellow in the top drawer.

II

Of course now she is older.
She can look in the mirror
while passing to her own face all the unused tenderness of hands that
never probed deep enough, her own.
She can handle things.
She can return manipulation gracefully.
She can pass judgment without hostility, of course,
and actually feel good about her "presence of mind."
She believes in the logical order of events:
chains are for punishment, tears for redemption.
She has a degree in plexi-glass frame over the mantlepiece,
a promising husband who definitely loves her
in "his way"
children with a future in the bank,
a past that doesn't scream
because it disintegrated behind locked doors
and elegant, Chinese screens,
a childhood pressed between family albums
a moderate imagination that doesn't take any leaps,
doesn't change seasons,
well-kept teeth that don't bite except in her dreams.
She is a lady now.
Her conscience has finally by-passed her needs.

She has disguised her life so well,
that nobody, not even she, notices it because
bleak vision means refinement,
There are no emergencies,
no veils to be lifted,
no edges on the periphery of time. No time.

III

She roamed the rooms in hateful resignation
and listened to the silence strike down
the echoes of her own heartbeat
one after the other.
Her wounds had been pawned for nothing
for a river that never overflowed,
an empty robe
a clumsy twist of the knife.

Night at the Opera
or The Exit of the Prima Donna

Withdrawal was dripping slowly on her sadness:
one, two, three drops of subdued instinct.
The polyphony of senses, loud and clear:
        The audience was listening.

Submission was dripping slowly on her wounds:
one, two, three drops of declawed passion.
The aria of mediocrity, quite effective:
        The audience got indignant.

Incongruity was dripping slowly on her endurance:
one, two, three drops of retired guilt.
The intermission of promises, rather bleak:
        The audience started to yawn.

Sleep sealed her choices:
many drops of damp defeat.
The leap of life, very spectacular.
        The audience was jubilant
for the "bloodless," "well poised death"
        of the primadonna.

Open to the Public

"No charge," the General had said,
e v e r y t h i n g for the people.

Dedication

Let the smell of your tender hands
touch my blood, as it slowly becomes acid,
among friends I never heard of,
with my nerves like razors
among trees made of fearful nights
and dark, dissonant sounds.
Let my words become the promise
I never gave you
when alive.

The Departure

To Vassili – In Memoriam (1942-1968)

So, you are gone,
young son of the tender lightning.
So, you are gone. . .

Distance, I used to tell you,
is nothing but a defined necessity for more love,
more kindness. . You remember?

Like a blue moment of freedom,
like a gentle swallow beating its frail wings
in the sun with joy,
you came and left from the huge stage
we perform each day
gracefully enough to cheat death.

Love, I used to tell you,
is nothing but a red wide sheet
carefully wrapped around each of us
with braveness, silently, yet loud enough
to awaken the sleeping conscience of the world. .
You remember?

You could smile
while blood was running down your dreams
– distorting them –
you could smile and hope.

This world, I used to tell you,
is our last chance for definitions and resurrection.
These people with the wounded hearts
and the open hands that are not ready to receive
a Sunday dressed charity,
were our last exit to light. . . You remember?

So, you are gone. . .
This life, you used to tell me,
will become a bright, colorful vestment of sensitivity someday. . .

Now, you are gone
and
I remember. . . .

The Reception

–He was lost last summer,
they say,
or was it this summer?

–It doesn't really matter,
please, continue. . .

–Somewhere away from home,
or was it at home he was lost?
Nothing exceptional, of course;
he trusted his country too much
and drowned in his own faith
–or was it in his country that he drowned?

–It doesn't really matter,
please, continue. . .

–He was young, you know
an irrational revolutionary like
most of "them," as they say. . .
He loved the pretty girl dancing with
the senile general, over there. . .

–How romantic,
life goes on. . .

–Doesn't it though? The silent man
with the black carnation on his heart,
is his father.
He was huge, they say,
but now he shrank
like light over dead light. . .

–Amazing; May I have
another drink?

–Certainly. It's free.
He can't speak any more, they say;
All he whispers is "why" and "hollow". . .

−You are so pleasant;
Are you married?

                  −Thank you, I am. Too bad I can't
                  recall his name, though;
                  −or was it taken away from him
                  before his life?

−It doesn't really matter,
please, continue. . .

                  −The veiled woman under the
                  framed photograph is his mother.
                  I'll have another drink, merci.
                  She is an artist, they say,
                  but now,
                  she only draws red horizontal lines
                  on white canvas.
                  Odd, is it not?

−Your story made me hungry;
shall we go?

                  −Allow me to escort you to his bedroom.
                  They say it's like the interior of his mind.
                  Dead people are remembered, of course,
                  of course,
                  but their beds remain empty,
                  ha-ha . .

           Oh, our condolence, Madame. . . .
           What a gorgeous evening!!!

"Open to the Public"

To the "happy" people of a "free" land.

It was there,
the naked anonymous body
dangling from the white rope
with serpentine agony
on the last Sunday of Carnival.

No charge, the General had said,
e v e r y t h i n g for the people.

Cities

I have seen too many cities late at night
—in moments of ultimate transformation—
or in the early morning
when sleep withdrew
   and burned, gray holes
   marked the instance of dreams.
Lonely cities, dark,
in spite of the lights and the ornaments
like old, abandoned whores
who do not deny anyone in order to exist
   with or without pay,
     with or without pride
      with or without

Just cities, still wet from the
     delayed tear of the
       torturer
who has finally justified
        death.

The Prize

The winners stood in line
reaching for the prize
    wine and sugar
     −as expected.
The winners looked around
(the crowd was silent)
and sugar had turned
into salt
     −not as expected.
The winners looked inside
  their fancy dressed-up
    triumph
(the crowd was silent)
and they reached out for
  the old agony
    of the new battle:
    salt and water,
    THEIR victory.

Signs

Be lenient with your love,
she said,
don't play it on the dice. . . .

Condemnation

"And all men kill the thing they love. . ."
                                   Oscar Wilde

The frame of isolation, painfully smooth
with worn out ornaments here and there.
The lack of hope, quite perceptible: some tears,
always escape from each man's condemnation
to the slow death of "dignity" or "self-sufficiency."
The merciless quietness of loneliness
binds me to my own breath:
My very voice rejects my declarations.
The sudden melting of my feeling into your deeper particles
turned the distance into intimacy;
my protective wall in ruins.
The taste of your absence
was that of decaying ecstasy between two people in love,
a false conception of survival against years
of rusty rules that, like nails, hold inner
emptiness in place with the rigidity of a dead dream
that exploded in its own one dimension, unseen.

Standing in the midst of my self-refusal,
I painted my needs with the dark color of fulfillment.
Then, I turned on the light,
stood motionless by my grief
and watched the burial of my emotions.

Navigable Mythology — V

(The cruel years — Awareness)

I have identified with the parable of the absurd
        and I don't regret it.
Bending with humility over the mountains' wounds,
  my hurt is easily forgotten
  even by me,
the "twentieth century child of brine"
eternally in love with the sea's feminine rage.

I have a measuring cup in the pocket
  of my portable aloneness
made of shell and sand
to measure the tons of grief
  and the drops of reward . . . .
useless effort: I have always flunked
  my life's arithmetic
    (no talent for calculations)
  and I don't regret it.
I was good in the calisthenics of perception
  and I have not forgotten the pensive apostle
  who taught me the permeable anatomy of love,
  a fragile course,
    like paganism itself,
      like the teacher,
        like the student,
          like the inevitability of death . . . .

Now, at my twenty-fifth celebration of a mediocrity
  I do not regret,
(regretting is a form of estrangement
and I have had my share of oxidation already)
I find competition a matter of forced relevancy,
and relevancy, a matter of well organized submission,
  with overshadowed exits pointing to oblivion . . . .
I find it hard to apologize,
  easy to sink,
hard to erase,
  easy to die,
hard to request . . . .

When the music is over,
the fragmented dignity inhumanly erect,
the beloved eyes immobile behind
   the crystal frame of passivity,
the anonymity of conscience, tragically alert,
I might whisper calmly to myself in time,

   Yes, I do regret it . . . .

Exposure

Here is all of me:

My skin, not thick enough to repel its own image,
folded with care next to my bed but out of reach;
the nine-headed snake, hibernating where I used to keep my letters,
poisoned the past with invisible, consistent bites.
Dried pesticide all over the shelves
that aged with all the unread or misunderstood wisdom
piled volume after volume on my heart
that never understood anything but volume,
still, kept getting weaker and weaker inhaling all the outside resistance to volume,
fighting the loose connections of love
that lose themselves in non-committal endurance.

Here is half of me
with a bottle of black ink broken all over my mind once so clear,
holding on to boundaries without name or life
out of habitual fear or fearful habit,
without crossing the vagueness of their bridges
refusing the routine of playing despair like music
and knowing, always knowing where the other half is,
how to turn the borrowed key
and how to patch up my insubstantial pride.

Here is everything
written hurriedly in an enigmatic poem that meant to be fierce
printed on some kind of cheap, impersonal paper
while waiting for the overdue orders to arrive
with permanent addresses,
with roots
so I can wash the ink off my patience
without new blanks or old stains
to concentrate, with healed vision,
on playing the game again.

The Traffic of the Heart

We have forgotten the love that is nothing but love
and NOT blood that drips slowly from the unspoken promises
NOT indifference that lies awake like naked blade
NOT misty solitude around the trembling lines of hesitant hands
NOT cruel altars for instant sacrifices
NOT abusive force in spite of its force
NOT incoherent sounds but clear, persistent scream.
The love that is more than the merciless sea of separations
that moves faster than the anger of pain
that cannot be postponed for "better times"
–There are no better times except for these, here,
in this present sphere of madness–
that carves the body into millions of pieces
and throws them behind sealed doors and lowered eyelids,
THAT love, that is nothing but love
undefined like the fever of spring nights
and sleepless volcanoes that always explode without warning,
the love that penetrates the seasons and turns them
into perfectly sculptured years
without the bleak awareness of isolated days or nightmares of
being unable to escape suffocation
without direction because
underneath all the intrusions
    the machine guns
        the brutality of fear
            the endless violation of memory
                the distorted face, our own, in the mirror
THERE IS ONLY ONE HEART.

That love.

A Skin Line

Should we decide to draw a line
between our feelings and our destiny,
the line should be in red,
like an ostracized fallacy,
a spectacular fall
or a technically dyed-in-blue horror.
The line would never be straight,
our hopes would be drier than thirst,
our hands heavy with promises
tied in lachrymose knots.

A circus line,
a clown's moment of joy
wild and ephemeral,
a border line
narrow and stiff,
like the peace that clever politicians
prescribe in efficient lethargy
on death sheets
for leprosy and war
with their Sunday smile
and the expensive lavender on top of their sweat.

Where inner darkness
yields escape,
where weather changes
mark time's brutality
with happy spots of lambent
kindness,
where people reconcile their faith
with their beliefs,
and expose their nakedness to the dogs
with leniency,
there the line should be drawn
with coal,
marking destiny's caustic expansion
and time's capricious games.

Omens

There will be times when,
  the pages of your heart
will fill with omens that nobody
  will recognize.
Times when tears will be the only generosity
  you can afford against submission,
inexplorable, magnificent times
  of conscientious desire for more,
the more that lies beyond the eyes
  of the wounded,
more Life, more Life,
perhaps the undefinable more of the gods,
  Nectar and War,
the ecstasy of the primitive moon
as it slowly enters the womb of dawn
and more, and more without rest,
with the ripeness of the amber grapes
before they turn into liquid grief.

I still hold on to the hands of the willow;
  the roots of the rain we tamed,
move deeper and deeper into
  the quarries of Memory—
and the bitterness of absence,
anchored in the blue silence of the unknown . . .
Now, from the square windows we can see
  the shooting-range and the hospital,
  cold and grey in the agonizing dusk.
We spread our hopes on the wires
  to dry the blood from their veins,
and as we recall the white moments
  of pride and
the house on the shore with the
  crystalized form,
swords and messages from a suspended justice
crack the breasts of the night
  into galaxies of pain.

Procession

I am dying without anybody's permission
almost without choice
and I AM NOT READY.
This isn't the quick death I had so romantically hoped for,
the dignified, well-poised exit
but the slow, uncomfortable, ruthless process
of feeling everything and knowing nothing.
Facts have crippled vision
have demythologized illusions
have replaced fear with paranoia—
I can't even be the outsider I had wanted
to become (at the cost of my mobility)
My wildness on ice
My hands on ice
My body on ice
The phoney stillness of despair
sensibly curled up against your body
that lies alone in spite of my embrace.
Exploited strength
The inevitable heart concussion
caused by loyalty against resistance:
I will never resolve you.
I slip by, quick impression of motion,
changing my tradition of love
perpetual blister on your fate.

No mystery is left intact:
only suspicions.
I can't breathe anymore
I can't scream, I can't. . . .
I have seen the executioners
took them to bed for penitence
but they pulled the knife to my belly
and feasted on the scars.

Myth has healed the surface of blood
with infrequent tremors
volcanic secrets, dormant
between my eyes that resist their ash.

Oh, yes, I believe
I believe
I believe in everybody's good, "guilt-free" intentions
except my own
trapped in labyrinthine passages
blocked by expectations of steel
that amounted to nothing,
just like all the void promises,
metaphors, commitments
petrified and negated
but not forgotten.

I am a target in the eye of the wind
marked by my desire
to remain unchangeable
against all bruised-up dreams
and contradictions.

Wanted: Hope

In every action
every attempt
every banner that has been raised
by our inexperienced but wishful hands
declaring "freedom,"
there is always the last moment.

Between conception and truth
there is only one touch of the blade
we were given by our predecessors
against the shadows of doubt
and the comfort of self-pity:
The last moment.

Thrown against the current,
we insist on riding
the delusive reflection of a struggle
we never acknowledged as ours.
Others called it Hope.
We recognized it as
the last moment
and went with it.

...She Said...

Be lenient, she said.
The waves are high today
like your rage
and the moon caught the sky flu
so, no chance for light
these coming days.

Be lenient with your passion,
she said,
your eyes are not kind anymore
when you make your prophecies
for the returning soldiers
and the tide got stuck someplace,
out of time,
so, no chance for water
these coming days.

Be lenient with your hands,
she said,
they do not search for my body anymore
they only confirm their devouring
knowledge of its wounds
with delusive tenderness.

Be lenient with your destiny,
she said,
you no longer contemplate it dreamily
from the top of your discretion
but you spit on it instead,
and curse the openness of the restless ocean
that can't define Life for you.

Be lenient with your love,
she screamed,
don't play it on the dice...

But if you can't, she whispered,
cling to the trifoliate sadness
of your loser's skin
solemnly,
as if you were to make love
to a yielding reed...

Signs

For days and days
the sailing was uncertain.
The captain was silent
while playing solitaire at nights
and sipped the harshness of his drink slowly,
like flesh communion,
before he goes to bed
alone and naked.

"The maps are no good,"
he wrote his wife.
"The signs no longer mean hope,
the destination is blurred by the colors,
my myopia increased
and I have not been able to find
the golden Compass
in the linen closet."

The heat didn't really matter,
the sailors whispered,
as long as they could claim their
manliness again, after the fast's brutality,
on the thirtieth day.

"The boatswain cries all day in the sun,"
the captain wrote,
"He says the sea is hurting him.
He says the salt has slain his heart . .
The rats ate up our canned patience.
If I could only find the Compass."

It was a silent crash.
It was a tiny reef.
In the middle of the Women's Port,
the golden Compass sank last
on the thirtieth day.

Carmel by the Sea

Infinity explodes
into multitudes of wrinkled echoes
as the green, tolerant oceans
disclose their wavy secrets
under a sky of grief.

This scenery is too much
for our wounded eyes.
It has a blue that cries
a red that dies
hundreds of surrendered sea-gulls.

Pleasure (composed of gold-plated routines
and instant pain-killers)
framed in contemporary despair
decorates the walls of our impotent dreams
in rectangular shapes
—just the tombstone is missing.

Our pockets,
full of shells
and colorful wishes
stained with spots of dissatisfaction,
weigh like sacs of nothingness
made of faded skin:
that of our youth.
The human odor of burned waves
is the "spice of life."
Then, the salt dissolves in the abyss
like a promise from solitary lips.
The mountains smile knowingly
while their insides erupt in disapproval.
The salt
        white and sour
            like a fragmented kiss
                upon separation
                    before the dawn of again.

86

We kept our hands separate on the sandy surface.
Love, we said, should not become
our game today
because we used it so much
that the links were no longer shiny
and the sun was already descending
upon our beginning
with the remote redness of a farewell.
The road was bumpy
but the car was "made in Europe,"
and so we reached the top
with no damage
other than that of our heart's tires.
Desires were put aside
−no time for dessert yet−
and life became only
a question of healthy digestion.

The salt
    white and sour
        like a fragmented kiss
           upon separation
               before the dawn of again.

We lingered around the edge
taking pictures of the chaos
with all the prescribed reverence
−photography is a real art−
of the chapped lips,
of the invaded solitude. . .
There were two houses on top of the hill:
one, whose emblem was a dying eagle
−cheated pride, in black and white, is fantastic−
another, whose emblem was a breathing stone.
We stayed away from both
−no visits where we might be hurt−
listening to the extraordinary weeping of the dusk.

All dissolved,
disrobed
−in memory.

The sea gulls sang:

No more sky for us?

There goes a flying smile!
–Cameras are always late–
The wind stumbled on the invisible obstacle
of the deaf echo
that repeated monotonously:
"When do we begin to rest?"

No more sky for us?

And you, my love,
–no time to understand what I mean
when I say "my love"–
failed to see the blue missive I wrote in the dark
and had so carefully placed
next to your grief
against your empty hands.

It was all gone.
The road was suddenly too straight
and it was ending.
It was time for resurrection
or recrucifixion
–meals at 6:00–
or a drink in a crystal glass
–oblivion by the ocean is cheap
and you also enjoy the view
without stealing anybody's sadness–
nothing more
–personal feelings are not so important
in an expensive restaurant–
nothing more.

Human needs on sale that day
like the tickets of wisdom
we buy so cheaply from the cashiers of death.
No more waves licking our feet
no more miracles burning what is
already burned.
It was a reconciliated beginning
that nobody would care to finish.

All dissolved
disrobed
−in memory.
The salt
    white and sour
        like a fragmented kiss
           upon separation
                before the dawn of again.

Suddenly,
the star disappeared in
an envious void:
below us, no longer the ocean
but the abyss
surrounded the dizzy infinity
with precious, luminous dots.

                Carmel, California

For My Mother

My mother never asks why all the dead.

Portrait of My Mother

Now she listens to the echoes of summer
and tries not to cry while watering her plants at night,
while caressing our photographs in faded frames
that reconfirm our absence in their stillness,
while walking in the empty rooms
searching for more evidence of our having been there not too long ago,
a hidden ashtray, a sailboat, a stiff handkerchief,
of having been there,
crossing the endless miles, the fear and the heat
delaying death, her own,
removing the noose of defeat once more from her heart
serious, vulnerable, erect in her aged refinement,
she moves gracefully through the silence of her lowered eyelids.

Talisman of all times,
her pain engulfs silence, freezes it
simple, enigmatic and sharp
with a reasoning that surpasses absurdity
and abolishes judgment.
My mother never asks why all the dead.
In the forest of her memory,
she just remembers their wounds.
Behind her thick, dark glasses,
red geraniums sparkle. . .

Letter to My Mother

Dearest Mother,
when I think of it,
I didn't really choose to grow up so fast
even though you always said I was anxious
to ridicule the good fairies
who couldn't conquer the witch
or turn blood into rubies.
It happened as quickly as a flame turns cold
in exile,
then dreams of the fire and wants to come
back alive, but can't.
So much in me still unattended,
uncivilized, fierce,
wanting to resolve guilt, not postpone it
for another summer.
I won't have you for much longer.

Where does music go after sunset?
I still don't know, but I remember
how your eyes were always sad on Sunday
afternoons
carrying secrets, unspoken confessions and
a veil of melancholy that covered us all
" I won't go blind, I won't go blind,"
you said over and over,
but you did anyway,
even though you can still thread pain
through the eye of solitude
better and faster than anybody.

You say I don't write
but I do, I do,
I write poems you can't read
since you refused to learn the language
I speak for years now,
resenting it, but using it
to reduce the silence of anxiety and expectation.
You find my letters too dark or too red,
my voice hand-cuffed,
my answers, limited.
I do the best with my words, Mother:
they are my only capital.

Yes, I know
I left for two years
and I am still here
seventeen years older and later.

Distance has twisted both of my feet
so that neither fits here or there.
Here is a lot, but not enough.
There is everything I left,
taking a chance in permanence
and losing it.
The only thing that's permanent is change.
No matter how silent, how static your life is,
the soul accelerates its needs.

But distance is distance
and nobody likes it if you are gone too long
and pretend to belong.
I am tired of trying to belong.
The truth is
nobody ever does
although many outdo themselves
in adjusting to the worst, shaping it into
impressive clichés
such as causes, tranquility, nuclear family, love.

Your goals and objectives for a rewarding
life, please?

They pull out a list
much less detailed than the weekly grocery list:
This week's specials are:
Internal focus, excluding others
(special recipe from the analyst)
No crises (nothing too emotional, please;
There is not enough valium in the house)
    Weaving in and out of the real world
    (occupational therapy)
a more economical casserole for six
and, if nothing else interferes,
    bridge,
    tennis,
    trivia pursuit,

the P.T.A.
volunteer activities,
The Faculty Club,
The Trying to Find Your Identity Club,
maybe more openness
(what happens if we open too many windows?
Better give less and hope for more
than give more and get less).

Mother, I know it's anachronistic to dream in black
but there is no space for distorted colors.
The events leave us behind,
They forget us,
Youth turns to rust
and the security of our childhood
has long anchored itself in memory.

My whole life will always smell of lavender;
I will always want to escape Sundays
with their counterfeit anticipation
but in the core of my anger
tenderness, as you taught it to us, will always make me mellow.

My most valuable safe has been
that of your heart
that contains forty years' deposits
        no withdrawals
        and no regrets.

Miranda Cambanis was born in Greece in 1944.
She came to the United States 18 years ago and
presently lives in Chapel Hill, North Carolina.

Design by Georgann Eubanks, Wordworks
Typesetting by Liberated Types, Ltd.
Printed in an edition of one-thousand by
Braun-Brumfield, Ann Arbor, Michigan.